creating your perfect

WEDDING

creating your perfect
WEDDING

stylish ideas and step-by-step projects for a beautiful wedding

Lucinda Ganderton

with projects by **Sania Pell**

RYLAND
PETERS
& SMALL
LONDON NEW YORK

DESIGNER Sonya Nathoo
SENIOR EDITOR Annabel Morgan
PICTURE AND LOCATION RESEARCH
Emily Westlake
PRODUCTION Gemma Moules
ART DIRECTOR Gabriella Le Grazie
PUBLISHING DIRECTOR Alison Starling

First published in the US in 2005 by
Ryland Peters & Small
519 Broadway, 5th Floor
New York, NY 10012
www.rylandpeters.com

10 9 8 7 6 5 4 3

The ISBNs for this paperback edition are as follows:
ISBN-10: 1-84172-940-X
ISBN-13: 978-1-84172-940-4

Library of Congress Cataloging-in-Publication Data
Ganderton, Lucinda.
  Creating your perfect wedding : stylish ideas and step-by-
step projects for a beautiful wedding / Lucinda Ganderton,
with projects by Sania Pell.
    p. cm.
  ISBN 1-84597-064-0
  1. Handicraft. 2. Weddings–Equipment and supplies.
  3. Wedding
decorations. I. Pell, Sania. II. Title.
  TT149.G3584 2005
  745.594'1–dc22
                        2005013889

Printed and bound in China.

contents

Introduction

Every wedding is unique—a celebration of the romance between the bride and groom, and a joyful occasion when friends and family come together to share their mutual happiness. Whether you are planning a traditional, formal event with a grand reception, or a simple service with only a handful of people in attendance, your wedding should be enjoyable, memorable, and just as individual as you are.

Creating a perfect, magical wedding is not reliant upon unlimited funds or extravagant flourishes. Amidst all the ceremony, it will be the attention to detail that stands out and that will linger in the memory of your guests. Exercising your creativity on these fine details should be an enjoyable process and it's a compliment to everyone who attends your wedding to make the day as beautiful as it can be. There's no set formula for success. You can tailor your wedding to suit your taste and budget, even if much of the organization is being delegated to a wedding planner.

This book brings together a wealth of creative ideas, all of which will inspire you to add a personal touch to your festivities and to make your wedding day entirely your own. Along with the enchanting and easy-to-achieve step-by-step projects, there are pages of gorgeous flowers, suggestions for table settings, ideas for thoughtful favors and romantic keepsakes, and special souvenirs for you and your guests to treasure.

Wedding flowers

Flowers are a vital ingredient at any wedding—their colorful petals bring fragrance, drama, and a sense of romance to the celebration. There are so many beautiful blooms to choose from—delicate silky-petaled sweet peas, regal lilies, luscious full-blown roses, or dainty lily of the valley are just a few of the favorites. Whichever you pick, be sure to carry the theme from the bride's bouquet and the groom's boutonniere through to the table arrangements and chair backs at the reception.

ABOVE A domed bouquet
needs little extra adornment:
here, a luscious bow of bronze
satin provides the perfect foil
for a densely packed bunch
of yellow Illios roses.

RIGHT Pristine white roses
are complemented by swirling
loops of wire-edged gauzy
ribbon in a metallic bronze.

bridal bouquets

Whether the wedding theme is traditional, minimalist, formal, or casual, every
bride is certain to carry a bouquet on her wedding day. Dreamy, sensuous, and
fragrant, the bridal flowers should be an expression of their bearer's personality
as well as the perfect complement to her gown. As with wedding dresses,
fashions in bouquets have changed over the years. Looking back through
any family album will reveal structured, formal bouquets that can look stiff to
modern eyes. Contemporary bouquets tend to be more informal. They are
usually hand-tied and use a wider choice of flowers than ever before.

FAR LEFT Imported roses are now available all year round. For this autumnal bouquet they are combined with berries, oak leaves, and kumquats.

LEFT Delicate, fragrant lily of the valley is the most charming of all spring flowers. When grouped en masse, as here, the effect (and scent) is stunning. The flowers are encircled by their own glossy green leaves.

ABOVE The availability of tulips is also no longer restricted to a short flowering season: nowadays, their rich colors and perfect petals can brighten the cooler months, too.

ABOVE The very best fabric flowers are hard to distinguish from fresh blooms: the veining and shading on the petals and leaves of these pink roses is subtly authentic. A silk bouquet can be treasured for many years.

ABOVE RIGHT An old-fashioned favorite, anemones are now enjoying a revival. The shell-pink petals of this unusual variety contrast graphically with the charcoal centers, a color that is echoed in the lavish organza ribbon.

RIGHT All-white wedding flowers are a traditional choice, but this informal garden bouquet is unmistakably contemporary. The stems are bound with ribbon and secured with pearl-headed pins (as shown on pages 16–17).

FAR RIGHT This romantic round arrangement is assembled from a skillfully chosen mixture of flowers, which all fall within the same narrow color range. It is another example of the trend towards minimum foliage within a bouquet.

TOP The flowers in this sophisticated, structured bouquet were chosen for both their fragrance and their color: ranunculus, delicate sweet peas, and deep-red roses. Any extra foliage would have detracted from the effect.

ABOVE Here is a truly sentimental Victorian-style posy: according to *The Language of Flowers*, forget-me-nots embody "true love" and pansies "tender and pleasant thoughts."

RIGHT Yellow and purple oppose each other on the color spectrum, giving any arrangement that includes them an added vibrancy. This pairing of sunflowers and cornflowers is the perfect choice for a summer wedding.

FAR RIGHT Like other exotic blooms, these Singapore orchids have intensely colored, intricately shaped petals. Bunched together with a binding of ruffled satin ribbon, they make a tactile, eye-catching bouquet.

BELOW These purple and cream lilac branches will fill the air with their heady perfume. They are informally tied at the top with a wide satin ribbon, leaving the dark, woody stems uncovered.

A wedding bouquet is the one accessory no bride can be without.

Although wiring is still used to give some support, the structure now comes from the flowers and foliage themselves. As a rule, the more tailored the bridal outfit, the more structured the bouquet should be: a slinky sheath demands nothing more than a few exquisite blooms, while a full skirt is better balanced with the lush informality of a lavish bouquet.

Most species are now available all year round, but seasonal flowers have their own particular charm and, more prosaically, are less costly. Spring is a time for delicate, fragrant flowers, while summer offers a wealth of choice in myriad colors and shapes. Autumn and winter foliage is striking: copper beech, holly, berries, and ivy (whose tendrils represent "wedded love") will all complement a wide range of flowers.

THIS PICTURE Unlike its fragile cousins, the Iceland poppy is a robust cut flower that makes an exuberant, colorful, and unusual bouquet.

FAR LEFT A moss-filled rustic willow basket will keep its contents fresh throughout the long day and can be carried easily.

LEFT An appealing combination of lilies of the valley and sweet violets is given a new twist with trailing ribbons and sequins.

PROJECT 1
hand-tied bouquets

An arrangement of a single bloom has great impact, and these bouquets show the flowers off to their best advantage. Choose flowers with perfect petals and, if necessary, give the cut stems a quick blast with a hairdryer to prevent any sap from leaking. The stalks of the bridal bouquet are bound and pinned with ribbon, while the bridesmaid's flowers have been more informally tied with lace and velvet to complement her dress.

MATERIALS & EQUIPMENT

BRIDE'S BOUQUET
1 yard of 2$^{1}/_{2}$ in-wide satin ribbon
Pearl-headed pins • Floristry wire
Scissors • Flower shears

BRIDESMAID'S BOUQUET
12in of 2$^{1}/_{2}$ in-wide satin ribbon
12in of lace trim
18in of $^{1}/_{2}$ in-wide velvet ribbon
Pearl-headed pin • Matching bead
Scissors • Flower shears

1 Make sure the stems are clean, then carefully remove any thorns or surplus leaves (wearing gloves if necessary). Arrange the flowers in a domed bunch, holding them close to their heads, and bind the stems with wire.

2 Cut 8in of ribbon and fold under one end. Wrap it around the stems and pin in place, slanting the pin downward. Repeat four more times, overlapping each ribbon, and trim the stems in line with the bottom edge.

1 Hold the flowers in a bunch, just below their heads, and shape them into a rounded dome. Keeping them in this position, secure the stems with floristry wire or a piece of lace and trim the stems to the same length.

2 Place the strip of lace on the satin ribbon and wrap them around the stems. Pin the edges together at the back. Tie the velvet ribbon in a bow at the front. Thread the bead on the pin and push it through the knot to finish.

attendants' flowers

The flowers that the bridal attendants carry or wear should continue the overall theme of the wedding and harmonize with the bride's bouquet. The arrangements do not all have to be exactly the same, however—several different groupings of the same flowers will look more interesting than identical bouquets. When choosing the size and shape of their individual arrangements, bear in mind the age of the bridesmaids and flower girls. Grown-up attendants may be happy to hold a bouquet throughout the day, but little fingers tend to get fidgety. Consider tightly bound posies, baskets, floral hoops, or pompom-like flower balls as an option for the youngest flower girls.

TOP LEFT Bridesmaids' flowers need not always be on a smaller scale than the bride's bouquet. These complementary hand-tied bouquets for a bride and her attendant are distinguished by using different types of foliage for each one. The bridesmaid also has sprigs of jasmine pinned in her loosely flowing hair.

TOP CENTER A stylish and fashionable corsage for an attendant is created by stitching a single hydrangea head to a length of woven braid.

TOP RIGHT Blue and purple spring flowers—forget-me-nots and pansies—in a simple posy for an older attendant. Their intense color is emphasized by loops of shiny satin ribbon.

CENTER Daisies, with their attributes of beauty and innocence, have long been a favorite choice for younger attendants. The pink and white varieties used here have been combined with forget-me-nots to colorful effect.

BOTTOM LEFT Two delightful posies in spring shades of lime, apple, and yellow-green, framed with dark ivy. One is arranged in precise concentric rings, like a "tussie-mussie," while the other is a more haphazard grouping.

BOTTOM RIGHT Tiny flower girls should be given flowers that are easy to carry and relatively robust. These pompom-shaped hydrangea balls and matching circlets should withstand a modicum of wear and tear.

boutonnieres

Just as most brides carry a bouquet, the majority of grooms
sport a boutonniere in the lapel of their wedding suits. This
flower arrangement in miniature usually takes its cue from the
flowers that make up the bridal bouquet. The stems of the chosen
flowers are trimmed then bound with florist's tape, which can be
camouflaged with pretty ribbon or upholstery braid. A single rose
is the classic choice for a boutonniere, but there are a wealth
of other decorative possibilities that will look equally elegant.

ABOVE LEFT This combination of
yellow and white freesia and irises set
off by a spray of mimosa would bring a
breath of fresh air to a spring wedding.

ABOVE CENTER A demure little cluster
of grape hyacinths is reminiscent
of a Victorian posy. The flowers are
encircled with glossy galax leaves and
bound with a criss-crossed blue ribbon.

ABOVE RIGHT The bright yellow
centers of the tiny chamomile flowers
pick up the color of the tightly furled
petals of the ranunculus heads.

RIGHT The stem of this flawless pink-
edged Candy Bianca rosebud has been
bound with tape to conceal the wired
ivy leaf supports, then embellished with
a twirl of fine flowery upholstery braid.

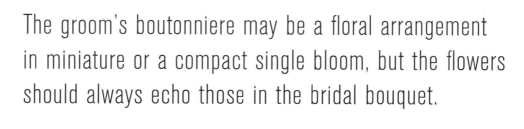
The groom's boutonniere may be a floral arrangement in miniature or a compact single bloom, but the flowers should always echo those in the bridal bouquet.

ABOVE LEFT If the bride is carrying an exotic bouquet, the groom's boutonniere can pick up on the same theme. Discreetly spectacular, this velvet-textured burnt-orange cockscomb makes a ruffled collar for a rich apricot rosebud.

ABOVE RIGHT Here, the groom's boutonniere (below) is fashioned from a luscious deep-red Grand Prix rose and a spray of winter jasmine trimmed with a toning satin bow. The other male members of the bridal party have boutonnieres that are a variation on the same color scheme, concocted from Martinique roses turned inside out and wrapped in galax leaves.

LEFT A single, perfect white rose is the traditional boutonniere. This one, with its petals just starting to unfurl, looks classically elegant against the dark suiting of the groom's lapel.

PROJECT 2
floral headpiece

This elegant confection is a stylish reworking of the traditional flowered headband and net veil combination. The headpiece would look perfect with either a formal or informal wedding outfit, and will complement any hairstyle—upswept or down, long or short. The delicate flowers are cut from paperlike silk taffeta (you could make them from remnants from the bride's dress), then trimmed with glittering rhinestones and threaded on crystal bead stamens and attached to a comb. The flirtatious net trimming and slender feather quills add a final flourish.

MATERIALS & EQUIPMENT
Tracing paper and pencil • Length of cream silk taffeta
or similar non-fraying fabric, approximately 16 x 18in
Scissors • 16 x ¼in stick-on rhinestones • Clear adhesive
Floristry wire • Wire cutters • 60 x ³⁄₈in glass beads
3 x 12in lilac feather quills
4 x 8in white feather quills
4in-wide clear plastic hair comb • 1 yard of ¼in-wide ribbon
Needle and sewing thread
8 x 12in rectangle of net with curved corners

1   Cut one large, six medium, and six small petals from your silk, using the template on page 111. Fold each in half, then into quarters and eighths, pressing along the creases. Snip the tip to make a hole. Glue one rhinestone to each petal.

2 Thread three glass beads onto an 8in length of wire. Pass the end back through the last two beads and twist it firmly beneath the beads. Make nineteen more stamens in the same way, then twist them together in four groups of five.

3 Assemble the petals into four flowers. Thread a stamen through the center of each. Hold the feathers along the back of the comb and bind the wires around the comb to attach the flowers, starting with the smallest.

4 Starting at the outside edge, wrap the ribbon neatly over and under the top of the comb, passing it below the flowers and in between the teeth to conceal the wire and quills. Trim any loose ends and stitch them down.

5 Position the net veil at the front of the comb, beneath the edge of the flowers. Sew the two corners down, then hand-stitch the net to the ribbon, working from the wrong side. Pleat the net as necessary to fit it all on the comb.

LEFT The silver flowerpot that holds these pale rosebuds perfectly complements the gilt-edged plates and elaborate cutlery.

BELOW A clear glass vase is an unobtrusive container that will not overpower a dreamy grouping of white and green flowers.

table flowers

The floral theme of a wedding is generally set by the bride's flowers. The flowers and colors of her bouquet will set the style for other flowers displayed at the reception. Whether the wedding is a formal sit-down meal, a relaxed buffet, or a country-style garden party, fresh flowers will add to the enjoyment of your guests and enhance the table settings.

Once you have decided on a general theme and color scheme for the wedding, your choice of flowers will follow on naturally. Before you start to plan the flowers in any detail, it's sensible to visit the location and take note of the size and proportions of the space, the number of tables, and the way in which you would like them to be set out on the day.

RIGHT Tiny sprays of silvery green foliage break up the solid mass of these closely packed rosebuds.

BELOW RIGHT Choosing the correct container is as important as selecting the right flowers. This pewter dish is ideal for a short-stemmed, domed group of pink roses and stephanotis.

BOTTOM RIGHT This shallow dish of cream roses and green lady's mantle makes a pretty, informal centerpiece, ideal for a summer wedding.

Floral centerpieces are the main focus of the tables your guests will dine at, but they should not be so large in scale or so dramatic that they block the view across the table or prevent guests from socializing. Tall, structured arrangements are very striking, and can transform even the humblest of settings, but they are best saved for a position where everyone can appreciate them—in alcoves or set on pedestals. Attractive architectural features, such as deep windowsills or ornate mantelpieces, are also ideal spots to position larger-scale displays.

BELOW This beautiful outdoor setting, surrounded by lawn and trees, requires little more embellishment than a few perfect hydrangea heads artlessly grouped in a plain glass vase, and a border of trailing ivy and eucharis lilies pinned to the edge of the table.

ABOVE RIGHT Single roses stand to attention in a row of bud vases. One will be positioned at each setting.

RIGHT The elegant, sculptural lines of these calla lilies are exploited by being arranged simply in a clear glass vase.

OPPOSITE, MAIN PICTURE A luscious sugar-pink peony and a full-blown rose in the same shade float ethereally within a glass globe. Goldfish bowls make spectacular centerpieces, and are also economical, requiring just a couple of perfect specimens to create a huge impact.

OPPOSITE, INSET A single rosebud sits in a tall, slender wineglass. This witty individual arrangement is repeated at every place setting.

LEFT An outside setting always demands informality: this spontaneous grouping of flowers and berries seems to spill out of its bucket container as it glows in the intense sunlight of a late-summer garden wedding.

BELOW Paper White narcissi and hyacinth heads create a delicate effect when arranged in whitewashed terra-cotta flowerpots. They bring an air of simplicity to the starched linen and silver-topped cruets of a formal table.

Your table flowers should take their cue from the size, shape, and number of tables. Round tables are ideally suited to one dramatic central arrangement, while rectangular tables can look very effective decorated with a dainty posy at each setting, which can double up as a favor or place-card holder. Take advantage of a single long trestle table by decorating it with a long line of vases of alternating sizes running down the center of the table. Good natural lighting is a bonus for a daytime reception, while an evening meal will benefit from carefully thought-out candlelight, which could be incorporated into the flower arrangements.

LEFT Nowadays, artificial flowers look just as good as the real thing, but they are much easier to care for and last a lot longer! Here, a single perfect silk bloom and a tightly furled bud welcome the guests to their places at the dining table.

BELOW An already romantic setting for an outdoor reception is given a fairy-tale quality by garlanding the rustic columns with ivy and roses. The red and green color scheme continues with the suitably low-level floral centerpiece.

Round tables are ideally suited to one dramatic central arrangement.

RIGHT An old wooden garden bench is dressed up with a generous cluster of pastel-colored roses, crab apples, feverfew, and other garden flowers.

CENTER RIGHT This garland has been created by bending flexible branches of golden mimosa into a circle and binding them together at intervals with florist's wire.

BELOW LEFT Ribbed green hosta leaves tenderly enfold old-fashioned pinks and summer roses. The posy is tied with satin ribbon and wired to a folding garden chair.

BELOW RIGHT This glorious chair-back wreath was made by wiring lengths of ivy and anemone heads onto a ready-made twig wreath, available from good florists. Match the ribbon to the color of the petals.

chair backs

Floral chair-back decorations are a charming finishing touch to a wedding reception, whether it is held indoors or outside. Small garlands, large hoops, or compact sprays can be used to adorn the back of every seat, or just those at the high table. Scented flowers will perfume the air throughout the meal, and add to the enjoyment of your guests. Make sure, however, that each arrangement is attached securely and positioned so that it will not become damaged when the occupant of the chair is seated.

ABOVE RIGHT This white card cornucopia (an ancient symbol of fertility) has been filled with evergreen foliage and feathery flower heads, and suspended by a cream ribbon.

RIGHT Elegant spindle-backed gilt chairs like these are easily obtained from rental companies. Make the bride and groom's seats stand out even more by adorning them with tumbling cascades of flowers.

PROJECT 3
wreath of flowers

This exuberant wreath is fashioned from greenish-pink hydrangeas and studded with sugar-pink roses. It is not too large or cumbersome, so it could be carried by a flower girl as an alternative to a posy, or used to decorate a door or windowframe. The wreath should ideally be made on the day so that the flowers retain their freshness, but if it has to be put together in advance, be sure to soak the floral foam ring in water for an hour first. At the end of the evening, the wreath can be put away in a cool place to dry out and become a long-lasting keepsake.

MATERIALS & EQUIPMENT
Floral foam ring, 12in in diameter
1¹/₂ yards of medium-width gauzy ribbon
Shears or heavy-duty scissors
10 hydrangea heads • 15 roses
About 30 large sequins, ⁵/₈in in diameter
Floristry wire • Wire cutters
15 silk or feather butterflies

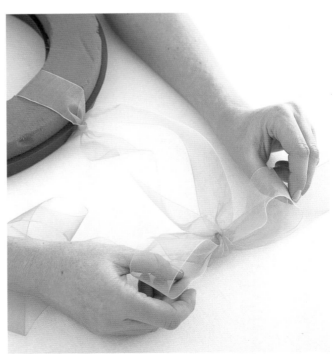

1   Slip the ribbon through the floral foam ring and knot in place, making sure the two ends are the same length. Tie them in a bow, 8in from the ring, adjusting the loops so they are equal, then trim the ends of the ribbon neatly.

2 Cut the hydrangeas into individual sprays, discarding any flowers that are damaged or discolored. Push the stalks into the floral foam, all around the ring, so that the flowers conceal the top and side edges of the ring completely.

3 Trim the rose stems down to about 5in and add them to the wreath, pushing them in between the hydrangeas. Arrange them in five evenly spaced groups of three to create maximum impact.

4 Position a sequin 1$\frac{1}{2}$in from the end of a 6in length of wire. Bend over the short end and twist around the long end. Do the same with the other sequins and add wires to the butterflies if they are not already wired.

5 Insert the wired butterflies at intervals around the edge of the garland, so they appear to be perching there. Push the sequin wires among the hydrangeas and roses in small clusters, so they catch the light as they move.

Wedding cakes

The traditional wedding cake, balanced on plaster pillars and topped with tiny figurines of the bride and groom, has in recent years been reworked into a delectable new confection of stacked tiers, fresh flowers, ribbons, and different flavors. But one thing will never change—the cake will always have pride of place at the wedding reception, where it is first displayed for the admiration of the guests, then later cut and shared among them.

The bride and groom cut the wedding cake together to symbolize their shared future.

LEFT AND CENTER LEFT Fresh flowers that tie in with the bride's bouquet can be used to add color instead of bright icing. Here, a posy of pink and red roses and purple lavender sits on each tier of this simple white cake, with a full-blown bloom perched at the very top.

BOTTOM LEFT In a radical departure from tradition, this cone-shaped cake is swathed with ruffled ribbons of glossy chocolate. Pastel flowers would be overwhelmed by such richness, so the cake is adorned with vivid pink, red, and blue anemones to create a bold effect.

A magnificent multi-tiered cake provides an important focal point at the wedding reception, and the ceremonial cutting of the cake is more than just another photo opportunity; like so many other wedding rituals, the wedding cake has a long history. It was traditionally baked from a rich mixture of exotic spices, nuts and dried "fruits of the earth" to represent fertility. Nowadays, wedding cakes come in every flavor imaginable, from plain vanilla through to carrot, lemon or even coffee, depending on the tastes of the bride and groom, while the frosting can be buttercream or fondant. Many brides still continue the custom of sending a small box of cake to those who were unable to attend the celebrations.

FAR LEFT White-on-white icing is elegant and understated. This brocade effect is created by piping small swirls and dots onto a smooth iced background, and the texture is emphasized by the bands of pearl-covered braid.

ABOVE Perfect pink hydrangeas and stephanotis decorate this layered cake. A dome of flowers caps the top tier, and posies cascade down one side. The icing pearls at the base of each tier contribute to the exquisite effect.

THIS PAGE One simple stacked cake is shown
two ways. Studded with artificial flowers and a
trailing organza bow, the cake has a softer look;
it appears more formal when decorated with
bands of wide satin ribbon (inset above).

BELOW LEFT This ultra-feminine confection in cool shades of shell pink is iced with an interwoven pattern and finished off with fresh roses, so that it resembles a stack of flower-filled baskets. The three square cakes can easily be cut into neat, evenly sized slices.

BELOW RIGHT Skillfully modeled sugar flowers, such as these naturalistic rosebuds complete with leaves, are almost indistinguishable from the real thing. They add a look of classic sophistication to a plain white-iced cake. A surprisingly wide range of molds and cutters to stamp out different-shaped leaves and petals can be found in specialty cake-making shops, along with ready-made icing for modeling, colorings, and stamens.

Such a gift can be particularly welcome: superstition has it that an unmarried girl who sleeps with the crumbs under her pillow will dream of her future husband.

Contemporary wedding cakes are varied and exciting. Not everybody has the same taste, and you may need to consider special dietary requirements, so cakes in which each tier is different are increasingly popular: you can pick and mix from lemon, chocolate, carrot or fat-free sponge cake, all of which can be decorated as you wish. Alternatively you could opt for a French croquembouche (a teetering pile of choux pastry buns), a pyramid of meringues, or—a key trend—individual cupcakes with bright icing or sugar flowers arranged on a tiered cakestand.

ABOVE LEFT, CENTER, AND RIGHT Each of the tiers that make up this gorgeous cake has been edged with rolled white chocolate as a delicious substitute for the more usual icing. The cake is topped with a ruffled chocolate rosette. The delicate butterfly ornaments that hover above each layer are the perfect finishing touches.

LEFT Tempting mouthfuls for the sweet of tooth: tiny petits fours in fluted paper cups can be piped with stripes, flowers, or a monogram. You may, however, need to allow more than one per guest, as they will undoubtedly prove irresistible.

RIGHT Individual cupcakes are an increasingly popular alternative to the conventional wedding cake. They can be iced with colors and motifs to fit in with any theme—these enticing versions are embellished with pastel hearts and flowers—then set out on a cakestand or large plate.

Superstition has it that an unmarried girl who sleeps with crumbs of wedding cake under her pillow will dream of her future husband.

Table settings

After the formality of the wedding ceremony, the reception is a time for festivity and entertainment. Family and friends have come to join together in celebration of your marriage, so create a welcoming atmosphere that lets your guests know how much you appreciate their presence. The wedding meal should be a visual delight, so plan beautifully decorated tables adorned with details that they will enjoy throughout the celebration.

Classic white napkins are the ultimate table accessory, and can be dressed up or down to match the theme of any wedding.

THIS PAGE Mother-of-pearl buttons and tiny pearl beads, all in pure white, have been selected to complement the textured stitching on these embroidered cotton napkins.

napkins

White napery—the archaic term for tablecloths and napkins—is a traditional choice for weddings. Crisply starched linen or self-patterned damask provides the perfect backdrop for flatware, china, flowers, and glassware, preventing the table from appearing cluttered. For effect, colored napkins, especially those in pastel shades, are a good way of picking up the wedding color scheme. The way in which the napkins are presented—rolled, folded, or tied—adds the final decorative flourish.

RIGHT These striking matt metallic napkin rings, constructed from coiled gilt wire, have been chosen to match a dinner service with a rich gold-coloured glaze.

ABOVE LEFT Tiny sprays of lavender, bound with raffia and tucked under bands of narrow organza ribbon, will release their scent as the napkins are unfolded.

ABOVE CENTER Hand-lettered name tags, made from simple rectangles of card stock, are tied onto silver filigree rings with short lengths of white velvet ribbon.

ABOVE RIGHT These loosely rolled napkins are bound with simple ties of gauzy ribbon. Use wire-edged organza, which retains its shape when twisted into knots.

Claudia

Most caterers will supply table linen as part of their package, but if you are having a wedding at home, or would like to provide your own linen, search for vintage napkins in flea markets and local auctions. Look out for pretty, unusual details, such as delicate lace edgings, embroidery, monograms, and hemstitching. Linen and cotton napkins can be restored to pristine whiteness by boil-washing and starching: old linen always improves with laundering, which enhances the texture of the fine fabric.

TOP Three ways with a hemstitched napkin: folded in half then pleated and tied with velvet ribbon; rolled up and secured with a fabric rose hair-elastic; and folded into thirds then pressed, with the place card slipped under the top layer.

ABOVE LEFT A napkin folded into quarters and tied at the corner with velvet ribbon holds a spray of autumn berries.

LEFT Porcelain napkin rings are paired with fine damask at the bride and groom's settings.

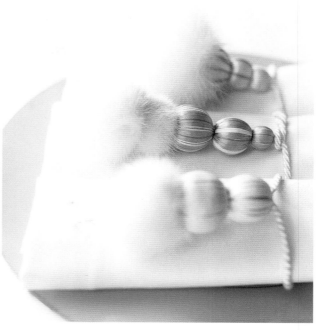

ABOVE LEFT Choose plain napkins and accessorize them with individual ties to set off beautiful china: this silver bead and rhinestone tassel is the perfect foil for a delicate silver-edged plate.

ABOVE RIGHT Scour sewing notions stores and furnishing departments for trims and tassels that can double up as quirky napkin ties. The fur trim on these elegant examples would add glamour to a winter wedding.

LEFT Another tiny dessert napkin— this time a fine linen square with a prettily scalloped edge—is cinched with a neat circle of embroidered Petersham ribbon. Use woven upholstery braid for a similar effect.

FAR LEFT After the main meal comes the ceremonial cutting of the cake. Provide guests with a pie fork and a fresh napkin, held together with a band of pink ribbon.

RIGHT Reminiscent of a more elegant era, a floral china cup and saucer complete with dainty lace-edged napkin set the scene for coffee and petits fours.

ABOVE A thrift-store find, this linen napkin is decorated with spring flowers. Search for similar napkins to set out on cake or dessert plates. They don't all have to be the same—quirky mismatching napkins look very cute.

Rules of etiquette dictate that the more formal the occasion, the larger the napkins should be. Some antique examples are up to three feet square in size. Often these were folded into intricate shapes—fans, lilies, or, especially for weddings, lovers' knots. Once the guests were seated, the napkins were unfolded and refolded across the lap, so a double layer of fabric protected the diner's clothing—still an important consideration today, when guests are all dressed up in their finery. Provide a few spare napkins in case of accidents, particularly for a buffet meal.

RIGHT Sets of monogrammed linen were once painstakingly stitched by brides-to-be as part of their trousseau. If you have the skill and the time, you could sew initials on your own napkins. Alternatively, if you're feeling extravagant, commission a monogram from a commercial machine embroiderer.

BELOW LEFT The unassuming elegance of white-on-white embroidery speaks for itself and needs little in the way of further embellishment.

BELOW CENTER A special decorative touch for the top table, maybe—sew a sprinkling of tiny ribbon flowers to one corner of a white napkin and display it in a wineglass.

BELOW RIGHT A border of buttonhole hemstitch adds color to a plain napkin, echoing the blue edging on the flower-sprigged plate and saucer.

PROJECT 4
heart-shaped napkin tags

Napkins are the finishing touch to a celebratory table laden with china, flowers, and sparking glassware. This simple project sees napkins secured with narrow ribbon and a handmade heart-shaped tag that has been decorated with vintage buttons or a delicate lace effect. The pretty tags also double as wedding favors. They are made from air-drying clay, which dries to soft gray-white, but the tags could be painted with acrylic craft paints to match your wedding color scheme.

MATERIALS & EQUIPMENT
Air-drying or oven-hardening modeling clay
Rolling pin • Pastry board
Scraps of textured lace • Heart-shaped cookie cutter
Selection of old buttons • Small leaves
Tapestry needle
Baking parchment • Cake rack
Fine sandpaper
16in length of ribbon for each heart

1 Roll out some of the clay on the pastry board to a thickness of around ¼in. Position the lace over the top and press it down gently with the rolling pin. Peel back the lace to reveal the texture and cut out heart shapes with the cutter.

2 Roll out the remaining clay and cut more hearts. Carefully press one or two buttons or a small leaf into the middle of each one. Using the needle, pierce a hole, just big enough for the ribbon to go through, at the center top.

3 Lift up the hearts carefully and place them on a sheet of baking parchment. Let them dry or bake them in the oven if necessary, following the manufacturer's instructions. Once dry or cool, smooth any rough edges with sandpaper.

4 Thread a length of ribbon through each of the finished hearts. Fold a napkin in half and roll it up tightly lengthwise. Tie the ribbon around the middle of the napkin and keep it in place by making the ends into a small bow.

ABOVE LEFT A small rectangular place card has been fixed to each of these cosmos daisies with a twist of florist's wire. The flowers have been placed in shot glasses and arranged in neat rows for easy identification.

ABOVE RIGHT Gold butterflies clip hand-finished paper leaves to an ivy garland. If, like this, your seating plan is to be hung up, allow space for your guests to gather around it.

place cards

A carefully thought-out seating plan is essential to the smooth running of any formal sit-down meal, but trying to work out the logistics of who should sit where can prove unexpectedly complicated. Give members of both families the opportunity to get to know each other, but remember that work colleagues, old friends, and distant relatives may prefer to sit with each other.

To help your guests find their seats, you will need to display a seating plan—a list pinned to the wall or a framed chart on an easel. If you want something different, opt for small envelopes bearing the name of each guest with their table number written

LEFT Tie a place card to a spoon, all ready for afternoon tea or after-dinner coffee. The cups and saucers can be placed on the dining tables or arranged on a side table for after the meal.

OPPOSITE Serried ranks of cute white baby squashes add laid-back country style to an autumn wedding. Tiny slits have been made in each stalk to hold the handwritten place cards.

ABOVE A foretaste of the feasting to come: a computer-printed name card is tied to spears of asparagus and balanced atop a wineglass at each place.

ABOVE RIGHT Place-card holders are found in many stationers or gift shops and can double up as favors. This porcelain bunny is an unforgettable keepsake.

BELOW RIGHT Classic white tent-fold cards such as this one are available from stationers. If you want to jazz them up, try using colored ink to write the names.

on a card inside. These can look extremely stylish when arranged in neat symmetrical rows on a table top.

At each setting, you'll need to display a place card. The traditional choice is a simple white card, but if you prefer, have fun with pastel shades or bold colors that tie in with your wedding color scheme. If you have attractive handwriting, you could write the cards yourself. Alternatively, consider commisioning a calligrapher to pen the cards. Nowadays computers have a good choice of fonts, and their printouts are quick, cheap, and easy to correct. You can even use the same font for the menus.

ABOVE LEFT Labeled wedding favors can double up as place cards. Here, enticing little favor boxes are tied with gold ribbon to match the plates and positioned at each setting.

TOP RIGHT Vivid red currants in white muffin cups make a striking visual statement. Tuck the name labels in among the berries.

ABOVE RIGHT Understatedly elegant, a handwritten name card is tucked inside an exquisite embossed teacup at each setting.

PROJECT 5
pebble place cards

These smooth, matt pebbles with a pleasing chalky texture make a novel alternative to the traditional place card (the pebbles can be found at garden centers or ordered from florists). Each guest's name and table number is added to a pebble, then they can be arranged on large trays or platters, either arranged alphabetically or by table. Guests can then find their own pebble as they enter the reception room. If you are short of time, you can speed up the manufacturing process by buying wire that comes ready-threaded with glass beads.

MATERIALS & EQUIPMENT
Medium-sized white pebbles
Flexible medium-gauge dark-colored wire
Wire cutters • Self-adhesive dots • Buttons
Sheet of rub-down letters and numbers • Pencil
Fine wire, such as floristry wire
Crystal beads, around 25 for each pebble
Small parcel labels or heart-shaped tags
¹/₈in-wide satin ribbon
Tiny silk flowers

1   Cut a length of wire, approximately 24in long, and attach one end to the underside of a pebble with an adhesive dot.

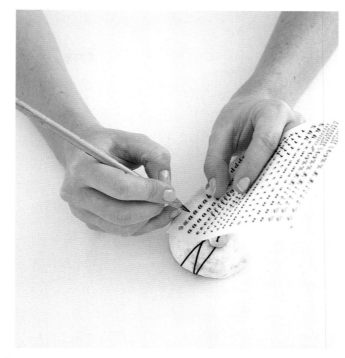

2 Wrap the wire once around the pebble and then thread it through one of the decorative buttons. Take it back around the pebble once more, trim the end, and anchor it to the underside using another adhesive dot.

3 Rub down the letters of your chosen name centrally onto the pebble, taking care to space them evenly. Following the seating plan carefully, add the guest's table number to the pebble on the other side of the wire.

4 Alternatively, secure a 24in length of fine wire to a pebble as before and thread on about 25 crystal beads. Wrap the wire around the pebble, sliding the beads to the top, and anchor the end to the underside with an adhesive dot.

5 Write the guest's name on one small tag and his or her table number on another, either by hand or with rub-down letters. Thread the tags on a length of ribbon and tie it around the pebble. Finish off by tucking two silk flowers under the wire.

centerpieces

Table centerpieces don't have to consist of the traditional floral arrangements. An imaginative or quirky arrangement will prove a good conversation starter as your guests are seated. Many-tiered cakestands, glass compotes, and old-fashioned etageres with two or three levels were all designed for display and look impressive when bedecked with fruit, bonbons, cakes, or cookies. If you're sticking to a tight budget, you could even forgo expensive floral arrangements in favor of a cakestand holding cookies or petits fours for guests to enjoy with their coffee.

ABOVE LEFT Roll firm, fresh fruit in beaten egg white and then in superfine sugar to give it a frosted finish, but warn your guests that it is purely decorative, and not to be eaten!

LEFT Metallic craft paint has been used to write the table number on one of the blown glass balls piled on this glass stand. Bunches of fresh grapes set among them add a slightly Bacchanalian air to the festivities.

RIGHT Sitting like a swan in a sea of Jordan almonds, this table number is made from silver beads threaded onto pliable wire and bent gently into a "2" shape. Its height makes it easy to identify from a distance.

FAR RIGHT A tiered cakestand can be set in the middle of the table to allow guests to reach out for handmade chocolate truffles to accompany cups of after-dinner coffee.

An imaginative or quirky arrangement will prove a good conversation starter.

RIGHT These Jordan almonds in a Victorian fluted compote tie in to a sophisticated silver and white color scheme.

FAR RIGHT Dainty decorated cookies are arranged on a tiered glass cakestand. The enticing goodies can be enjoyed with tea or coffee after dinner has ended.

PROJECT 6
chair cover

An ordinary wooden dining chair can be transformed into something special by concealing it with this simple slipcover, made from a combination of plain linen and pretty faded chintz. Sew a chair cover both for the bride and groom, and decorate them with either their initials or a monogram embroidered on the back. You do not need to be an experienced upholsterer to make this project, so don't be deterred by its professional appearance: the cover is not fitted to the chair, and since the linen drapes softly over the seat, there are no curved seams.

MATERIALS & EQUIPMENT
Tape measure • Scissors • Ruler and pencil
Squared pattern paper
20in square of flowered fabric
1⅝ yards of 20in-wide white linen or cotton
Sewing machine
Colored sewing thread or embroidery thread
Dressmaker's pins • Sewing needle
Matching sewing thread
2 yards of ⅝in-wide satin ribbon to match flowered fabric

1   Measure up the chair. Add a 1½in seam allowance to each panel. You need a panel for the back, one for the front, two side and one front skirt panels, and the seat. Add 2in to the back and front panels for the depth of the chair back.

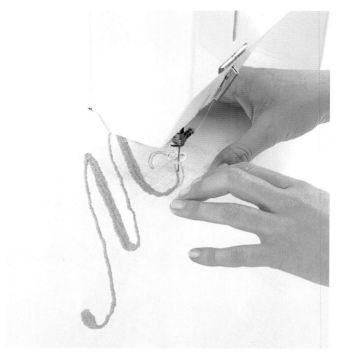

2   Transfer the measurements to the pattern paper and cut out the templates, labeling each one. Check the sizes against the chair and adjust as necessary. Cut out the chair seat from flowered fabric and the other pieces from plain linen.

3   Trace the outline of your chosen monogram on the front panel and embroider the letter by hand or machine. Fit an embroidery foot if you have one and work in satin stitch in a color to match the floral fabric.

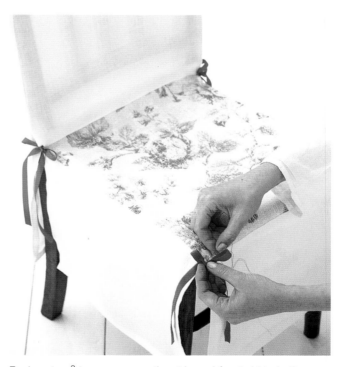

4   With right sides together, pin the front and back panels together and slip over the chair. Pin on the seat and the skirt to check the fit. Hem along the sides and bottom of the skirt panels and the lower part of the back.

5   Leaving ¾in seams, sew the side and front skirts to the seat. Stitch the seat to the lower edge of the front panel. Sew the long back to the front, turn inside out, and press. Make four ribbon bows and stitch to each corner of the seat.

Candles

The flickering flames and soft shadows of candlelight add an air of enchantment and intimacy to any event, thus making it the perfect addition to your wedding party. Whether you opt for classic many-branched candelabra, tall ivory-hued pillars, slender tapers, or simple tealights in glass jars, the tiny flames, with their warmth and romantic glow, will inevitably cast their spell over your guests.

ABOVE LEFT A simple centerpiece is created by a cream pillar candle on a fluted cake stand, surrounded by a handful of rose petals and fragrant white jasmine flowers.

ABOVE RIGHT This eclectic gathering of pressed-glass tumblers and engraved wineglasses reflects the soft light cast by the candles. Twist crystal beads onto silver craft wire to make sparkling garlands like those that surround the pillar and votive candles.

The romantic atmosphere created by candles will enhance any reception, whether it is held indoors or outside, and whatever the surroundings. Silver candelabra can be found at the middle of traditional table arrangements, while individual votive holders at each place setting are less formal. Groups of candles always look stunning, and can be set on side tables, used as centerpieces, or arranged on mantelpieces or windowsills. A word of warning, however: lighted candles must be placed safely out of harm's way and should never be left unattended.

LEFT Larger candles, which have two or more wicks to ensure even burning, make bright focal points for centerpieces like this garland of ivy and leaf-shaped name cards.

ABOVE A handful of tapers emerge from a froth of cow parsley and white nerines. The tapers are inserted into a block of wet florist's foam, which holds them securely in place.

BELOW Bowls of floating candles make eye-catching centerpieces. Pale pink candles have been chosen to complement the red roses and blush-colored petals that float alongside.

RIGHT Single lily heads drift alongside lighted white candles in a simple porcelain bowl. They create an ethereal feeling of calm and tranquility within an all-white table scheme.

BELOW This smaller group features just three floating candles, set amidst scattered rose petals in a shallow bowl. The soft glow of the flames casts patterned shadows through the glass bowl and onto the tablecloth below.

ABOVE RIGHT Arranging a multitude of candles on a reflective surface—a mirror or polished silver tray—is a simple and inexpensive idea that creates maximum impact. Faceted or embossed glass tealight holders, like these ones, add to the glittering effect.

RIGHT Create a sense of height by using tall candelbra, or by arranging votive candles on a tiered cake stand. Used singly, these ribbed, frosted glass votive holders are pretty, but when many are grouped together the overall effect is spectacular. The paper-lace doily, reminiscent of afternoon tea, is a delicate finishing touch.

ABOVE LEFT Turn an ordinary beaded votive holder into a hanging lantern by tying both ends of a length of ribbon to the top rim. These bejeweled versions are suspended from the canopy of a weeping willow.

ABOVE RIGHT Suspended in mid air, these delicate blown glass globes look like soap bubbles floating serenely past. Always make sure that candles are firmly secured within their holders by using special pliable wax or a blob of molten wax from a lit candle.

LEFT Light your guests' way with a row of tealights, placed at intervals along a path or terrace. These votive holders have been decorated with evergreen leaves and berries.

ABOVE LEFT The lace-like dome and panels of this pierced-tin lantern are specially intended to cast decorative shadows. Look out for similar Moroccan-style lanterns at stores that specialize in ethnic accessories.

ABOVE CENTER Chandelier-like crystal drops dangle from this decorative wirework votive holder. For a summer wedding out of doors, dot a series of lanterns around the garden for your guests to discover as twilight falls.

ABOVE RIGHT White risotto rice (a suitably bridal choice) has been used to fill a simple glass vase and support a pillar candle. Dishwasher salt or glass pebbles are good alternatives. A tall-sided vase or hurricane lantern is a sensible choice for an outdoor location, as the glass will protect both the flame and your guests from mishaps.

LEFT A row of concertina lanterns illuminates a garlanded arbor late into the night, creating the perfect setting for a summer party.

PROJECT 7
glass-jar candleholders

With a little glitter and glue, glass food jars can easily be transformed into glamorous, sparkly tealight holders. Collect a variety of different-sized jars, then decorate them with a scattering of glitter, beads, and rhinestones in delicate toning colors. The candleholders look fabulous arranged in clusters, in a row along a mantelpiece or windowsill, or encircling the centerpieces on the dining tables. You could even make one for each setting, and they can double as favors. Be safety-conscious—never leave a burning candle unattended.

MATERIALS & EQUIPMENT
Glass jars in a variety of different sizes
Assortment of glass beads
Fine wire • Wire cutters
PVA adhesive • Tweezers
Stick-on rhinestones
Glitter • Saucer • Tealights

1 Wrap one end of a 30in length of wire once around the rim of the jar and secure. Thread on about 50 beads and spiral the wire along the ridges of the screw top, spacing out the beads. Twist and clip the ends of the wire.

2 Decorate the jar with a sprinkling of rhinestones. Apply a tiny dab of glue to the back of a rhinestone and leave it until nearly dry. Pick up a stone with tweezers or press it on to the tip of your finger, then push it firmly onto the glass.

3 For an alternative effect, decorate the rims of the jars with glitter. Apply an even coating of glue all around the outside of the screw top and let it dry slightly.

4 Pour the glitter into a saucer, then dunk the jar in the glitter so the glue is completely covered all over. Leave until the glue is quite dry. If the coating is not even, add glue to the patchy areas and dip the jar again until the rim is concealed.

Wedding favors

The custom of presenting wedding guests with favors—
small keepsakes or delicious edible treats in gorgeous
wrappings—is a long-established and popular tradition.
Whether you place a pretty package at each table setting
to make everybody feel personally welcome, or distribute
them as parting gifts as your guests leave the reception,
these charming little gifts act as gracious tokens of
thanks, appreciation, and mutual celebration.

LEFT Sugar-frosted amaretti, an Italian favorite, go perfectly with after-dinner drinks. Here they have been packaged in a simple Cellophane bag with a knot of blue ribbon, placed in cups and saucers, then set out in rows on a side table. Tiny macaroons, biscotti, or gingerbread cookies could be presented in a similar way.

BELOW Part of a gold and white setting, these foil-covered chocolate hearts look sophisticated in a gold-rimmed champagne glass.

edible favors

Sweet favors are always popular. Silvered or pastel Jordan almonds are the traditional wedding choice, but individually wrapped crystallized fruit, truffles, or colorful candies are all excellent alternatives. Favor packaging need not be elaborate or expensive: iced cookies or foil-wrapped candies can be wrapped in tissue paper or Cellophane and tied with ribbon. While other favors are intended as souvenirs, these mouth-watering treats are offered as an accompaniment to coffee and liqueurs at the end of the meal—if your guests can wait!

LEFT If time is at a premium (and your budget allows), search for a specialty manufacturer who can supply ready-packaged candies, like this charmingly old-fashioned box of chocolate rose creams. You can then add a personal touch with ribbon, silk flowers, or a paper lace doily to fit in with the rest of your table setting.

BELOW Colored frosting and a fine nozzle were used to pipe names on to these rectangular cookies, giving them an extra role as edible place cards. They have been arranged around a table number made from blue glass beads threaded onto florist's wire and bent into a "5." Delicate bows to match the icing add the final touch.

Irresistible edible favors will add a dash of color, flavor, and fun to the reception table.

Guests of all ages will be delighted by these truly scrumptious treats.

FAR LEFT To save time, go for instant packaging. Fill clear plastic boxes with pastel-colored candies and tie them up with ribbon bows.

CENTER LEFT Cellophane cones are filled with white jellybeans and tied with sage-green ribbon. Jordan almonds would work equally well.

LEFT Little bundles of Jordan almonds have been presented to wedding guests for centuries, as tokens of thanks and good fortune. In Italy, brides wrap five Jordan almonds in net to symbolize the five qualities that contribute to a lasting and happy marriage: health, wealth, fertility, happiness, and long life.

LEFT Three variations on a pink and white theme prove the versatility of edible favors: a bag of gold hearts wrapped in Cellophane is tied with a gauzy bow, while white Jordan almonds look good in a tissue-lined box or tied with a polka dot ribbon.

ABOVE LEFT Tempting pink truffles are too pretty to hide away in a box.

ABOVE RIGHT AND TOP On a more fanciful note, at a late summer wedding a whimsical arrangement of beribboned baby pumpkins looks good enough to eat!

RIGHT Fine green ribbon, in a shade that exactly matches the enchanting fresh rosebuds, is used to tie up these white gift boxes and to secure the name tags. Make sure that the buds are added at the very last minute, so that they do not wilt.

BELOW LEFT Bundles of slender hand-dipped candles make a lasting memento that need no further adornment than a simple silver-gray cord tie.

BELOW RIGHT Subtly wrapped packages will intrigue your guests. These transparent glassine envelopes contain fine scented soaps, but could equally well be used to package a sachet of dried lavender, spicy potpourri, or a scented candle.

non-edible favors

The content of these pretty packages will depend very much on your budget and personal taste. Favors do not have to be expensive (particularly if you have a lot of guests), so use your imagination and have fun selecting something to please your friends and family. A packet of seeds or a bulb in a miniature terra-cotta pot, a hand-written verse or a votive holder are good for those on a tight budget. Other ingenious ideas include a CD of the music played during the service, a slim volume of poetry, or a scented candle.

ABOVE LEFT Bright ribbons bring color to a stack of square boxes. Choose stripes, checks, velvet, and ombré ribbons in matching shades.

ABOVE RIGHT AND RIGHT Fill envelopes with flower seeds, add a card with planting instructions and tie with a matching ribbon bow.

ABOVE Keeping to shades of just one color will always create a glamorous, grown-up effect. Here, a sheer burgundy ribbon has been used to tie a pale pink rose to a deeper pink favor box.

ABOVE RIGHT This picot-edged braid was carefully chosen to enhance the shade of the engraved blue wineglass. A place card has been slipped under the bow so that the place setting is easy to locate.

RIGHT Another single-color favor, this time in ethereal shades of cream: a silk flower corsage in a translucent onyx bowl adds a romantic and dreamy atmosphere to the dining table.

INSET RIGHT Twist faceted crystals onto fine craft wire to create a pliable garland to wrap around a packaged favor. Clear and green glass beads threaded on silver wire have been used to carry through the green and pink color scheme of this wedding reception.

ABOVE LEFT AND CENTER A dainty, decorative handkerchief makes an unusual substitute for wrapping paper, and is a lasting favor in itself. Look out for a lawn square or Irish linen with hemstitched borders or flower-sprigged embroidery. Place a small favor in the center, then tie the corners with a velvet ribbon or twist of wire disguised with a silk flower.

ABOVE RIGHT A couple with a shared love of gardening might opt for a miniature galvanized bucket filled with grape hyacinths and accessorized with a flower-fairy-sized fork. Once planted outside, these will come up year after year as a reminder of the happy occasion.

LEFT Nowadays, artificial fabric flowers are almost indistinguishable from the real thing. To adorn an extravagant gold-colored favor box, choose a decorative bloom that matches the bride's bouquet or the table flowers .

PROJECT 8
lavender hearts

These dainty lavender bag favors are guaranteed to enchant your guests. They are a special keepsake, and the evocative scent of the lavender that fills them will remind guests of your wedding day. If you prefer, you could fill the hearts with potpourri, dried rosebuds, or other fragrant petals: the muted color of the flowers will show prettily through the delicate organza. The hearts are decorated with simple embroidery and felt flowers, circles of Indian shisha mirror glass, and sequins, and finished off with a hanging loop of narrow braid.

MATERIALS & EQUIPMENT
For each heart:
6 x 12in rectangle of sheer or opaque silk fabric
Tracing paper and pencil • Dressmaker's pins
Scissors • Pink and green felt
Stranded embroidery floss • Embroidery needle
Flower-shaped sequins • Pink and green sewing thread
12in of narrow braid • PVA adhesive
Rhinestones • Shisha mirrors • Lavender

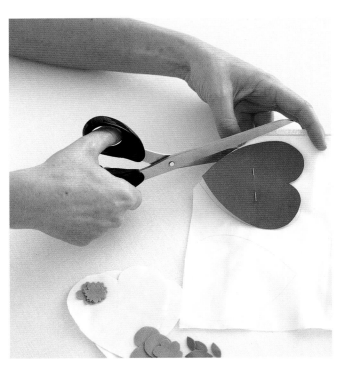

1   Trace the heart and flower templates on page 111. Use them as a guide to cut out two hearts from silk fabric and three pink felt flowers. Snip out six green felt petal shapes.

2 Thread a large-eyed needle with all six strands of a length of embroidery floss. Work a line of small, regular running stitches around the edge of one fabric heart, with a spiral at each end. This will be the front piece of the bag.

3 Arrange and pin the leaves and flowers to the front piece as shown. Anchor the flowers with flower-shaped sequins: work six straight stitches from the hole to the outside edge. Sew the leaves along the center spine with backstitch.

4 Fold the braid in half. Pin the two ends to the top of the front heart on the wrong side, then pin the back heart in place. Sew together around the outside edge, leaving a 1½in open gap. Fill the bag with lavender, then sew up the gap.

5 Glue a rhinestone close to the flowers with PVA adhesive. Make more bags in the same way, varying them by using sheer fabric, different braid, or adding darker flower centers and gluing on shisha mirrors alongside the rhinestones.

Finishing touches

Spend time and thought on planning the finishing touches for your wedding: it is these tiny details that will make the day unique. Here you'll find a wealth of beautiful ideas, ranging from confetti (to add a romantic touch to proceedings) to suggestions for thoughtful thank-you gifts that will delight your attendants. There's even a project for a handstitched ring pillow that will become an instant family heirloom.

confetti

As they cast handfuls of confetti over a newly married couple, wedding guests are unconsciously partaking in a ritual that dates back centuries. Today's bride and groom are likely to be showered with flower petals or delicate paper cutouts of hearts and horseshoes, but pagan couples were bombarded with rice or nuts, in the belief that the fertile seeds would ensure a prolific marriage. At a later date, these grains would be coated in sugar crystals and became known by the Italian term *confetti*, meaning "sweetmeats." Do check whether your wedding location welcomes paper confetti. Many no longer do, but dried or fresh rose and delphinium petals or even dried hops are an attractive biodegradable alternative, while the latest trend of blowing soap bubbles is exuberant, fun, and leaves no mess behind.

TOP LEFT At the exit from the ceremony, place a few simple wooden baskets filled with rice to encourage wedding guests to take part in an ancient tradition.

TOP CENTER Prepare fresh rose petals at the last minute so that they retain their scent and shape. Hold a rose head in one hand, then twist and pull the stem gently with the other, so that the bloom falls apart.

CENTER These tiny white petals will fall in a snow-like flurry.

BOTTOM LEFT Pure white daisy shapes are an attractive minimalist alternative to the multicolored pastels typical of most paper confetti.

TOP RIGHT Choose a pretty basket with an easy-to-hold handle for the bridesmaids or flower girls.

BOTTOM RIGHT An enamel bucket makes a more utilitarian container, but one that has its own quirky charm and is ideal for a simple country wedding. This one is filled with a combination of fragrant jasmine and rose petals.

A shower of confetti is a joyful symbol
of both fruitfulness and festivity.

ABOVE LEFT Simple white cartons can be
bought from wedding or stationery suppliers.
Simply fill them up with fresh petals, close the
lid, and tie a gauzy ribbon around each one.

ABOVE CENTER These origami-style folded
paper parcels are filled with rice and tied with
raffia knots. They are arranged on a bamboo
tray, ready to be distributed after the service:
a useful task for a young attendant to perform.

ABOVE RIGHT AND INSET OPPOSITE RIGHT
To form a confetti cone, fold over two sides
of a handmade paper square. Secure the edges
with paper glue or double-sided tape, then fill
the cone with pieces of torn paper and fabric
or real flower petals. Make one cone for each
guest and present them massed together
in a wicker basket.

RIGHT These dainty linen drawstring bags are
for the bride's attendants. Fill them with confetti
and hand them out before the ceremony.

TOP RIGHT Pearly grains of rice represent fertility and good fortune. Throwing them (gently!) at the bride and groom after the wedding ceremony is an ancient rite.

LEFT Embroidered sprays of lily of the valley decorate these confetti bags. Make them from a square of fine cotton, seamed at the side and bottom edges, then hemmed at the top and tied with a length of pretty ribbon.

gifts for attendants

Whatever the age of your bridesmaids, flower girls, or ring bearers, and whatever their role on the day, all your attendants deserve a special thank-you gift. Select each present carefully, finding something to match each person's tastes, then wrap them beautifully. Indulgent treats for your girlfriends might include a silver photo frame, a dainty evening bag, a bottle of their favorite perfume, or a charm bracelet. Younger attendants will be thrilled with a special story book, a toy, or even a "grown-up" watch or small piece of jewelry.

TOP RIGHT Variations on a theme: these sumptuous silk confetti bags make lasting souvenirs for bridesmaids or flower girls. Each one is embroidered with flowers or leaves, and has a cord drawstring closure.

BELOW Recreate this look by binding a box with a wide lilac ribbon, then tying longer lengths of gauze and satin ribbons over it and finishing with a bow. A velvet flower is the final flourish.

RIGHT Create this luxurious evening bag by folding a strip of brocade in half and seaming the side edges. Trim the top with marabou and tie it up with satin ribbon. Add another loop of ribbon so it can be hung from the wrist.

OPPOSITE, MAIN PICTURE Gift-wrapping does not have to be elaborate to be effective: here, crisp striped ribbons add a touch of drama to these small attendants' gift boxes.

OPPOSITE, LEFT AND CENTER These lustrous mother-of-pearl spoons and silver-topped shell boxes are an exquisite way to thank attendants.

OPPOSITE, RIGHT Metallic ribbons give a sophisticated finish to a gift. Fix each length to the underside with Scotch tape or a glue stick.

PROJECT 9
bridesmaid's bag

These pretty bridesmaids' bags are
easy to make and require only basic
sewing skills. Their quirky charm comes
from the numerous ribbons, buttons, and
beads with which they are embellished.
To achieve a similar vintage look, scour
flea markets or ask your friends and
relations to look in their sewing baskets
and donate any suitable trimmings.
Use a piece of linen or remnants of the
bridesmaids' dress fabric for the bags
and, for real individuality, make each one
slightly different.

MATERIALS & EQUIPMENT
Pieces of silk or similar fabric
Yardstick and dressmaker's chalk • Pinking shears
Iron • Stranded embroidery floss
Embroidery needle
Matching and contrasting sewing thread
Selection of pearl buttons and sequins
Dressmaker's pins • Sewing machine (optional)
18in length of medium-width ribbon or lace
Scraps of paper silk • Brooch back
16in of narrow ribbon

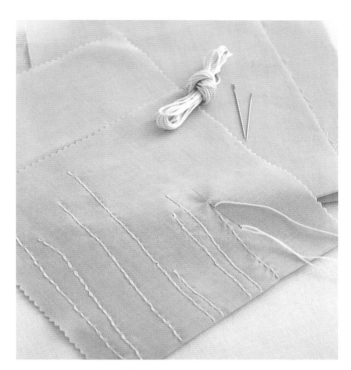

1 Using pinking shears, cut a 7 x 19in piece of fabric. Press under a 2½in flap at one short end, then fold the other short end up to the crease and press. Lay it flat and sew vertical lines of running stitch up the front of the bag.

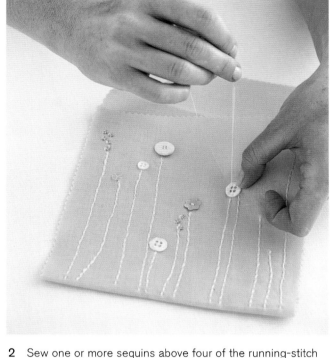

2 Sew one or more sequins above four of the running-stitch stalks to make a flower head. Stitch from the center to the rim in a star pattern. Pick out eight buttons in various sizes and sew them to the top of the remaining stalks.

3 With wrong sides together, pin the edges of the bag together. Pin one end of the lace or ribbon to each top corner, then stitch the seams, making sure the handle is secure. Hem the flap. Turn the bag right side out and press.

4 Using the template on page 111, cut three different-sized flower shapes from the silk. Stack them together and stitch through the center. Stitch the flower to the brooch back. Make bows from the narrow ribbon and sew to the corners.

RIGHT If you want to move away from a pale palette, go for taupe, which is always a good neutral background color and looks great with gold.

FAR RIGHT The satin top of this ivory bag is trimmed with insertion lace through which a fine cord has been threaded. An Oriental bead provides a "something old" fastening.

BELOW RIGHT An 8in length of upholstery braid is all you need for an edging, so you could opt for something wildly extravagant that would otherwise be prohibitively expensive.

BELOW This plump pillow is covered in a tactile bouclé fabric with a subtle looped braid along two side seams.

ring bags and pillows

The exchange of rings is the pivotal moment of the wedding ceremony, and one which is charged with symbolism and emotion. Safeguarding the two precious wedding bands and delivering them into the hands of the bride and groom is usually the responsibility of the best man, although at some weddings he will entrust them to a young ring bearer clutching a pillow just before the ceremony starts. Make sure that the rings do not go astray, by safeguarding them in a tiny bag, which can sit safely in a pocket. If your gown has been made to measure, ask the dressmaker for an offcut from which to make the bag. Alternatively, look out for luxurious fabrics, such as transparent organza, plush velvet, or pleated satin, and utilize pretty cords and ribbons for the drawstring.

THIS PAGE To make an unusual button into an eye-catching toggle, fold a 6-in length of cord in half and tie a loop $1\frac{1}{4}$in from the center. Sew the two loose ends to the back of the button, then slip the loop around the bag and over the button.

PROJECT 10
ring pillow

The heart-shaped pocket on the front of this dainty satin pillow will make it easy for even the youngest and most nervous ring bearer to perform the important task of looking after the two wedding bands. It will also alleviate the worries of the best man, as the rings are clearly visible at all times! Like the heart-shaped favors shown on page 82, this ring pillow is filled with dried lavender, so the evocative scent will fill the room as the rings are exchanged—the most important and moving moment in the wedding ceremony.

MATERIALS & EQUIPMENT
9 x 18in piece of white satin
Dressmaker's pins • Sewing needle
Sewing machine (optional)
White thread • Scissors
6in square of white organza • Red thread
Pearl button • 3/4in heart cut from red felt
Small white bow • Sheet of paper
1 yard of narrow decorative braid
Dried lavender

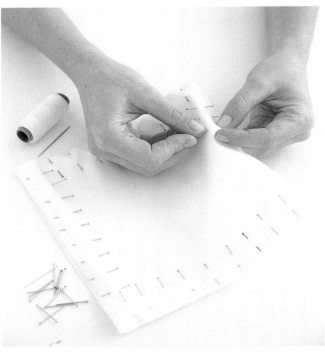

1   Cut two pieces of white satin, each 8 x 9in. Place them right sides together and pin around all four edges. Machine- or handstitch ½in from the edge, leaving a 1 ½in gap along one side. Turn right side out and press.

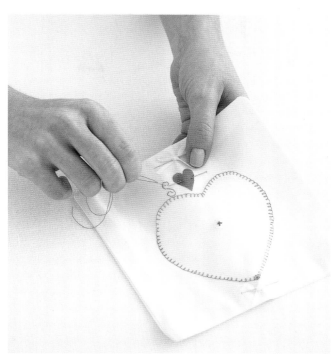

2 Cut a heart shape from the organza (using the template on page 111 if you wish). Thread a needle with a length of red thread and work a round of blanket stitch around the outside edge. Sew a button to the center of the heart.

3 Pin the heart to the front of the pillow and sew in place with more blanket stitches, leaving the top edge open. Pin and stitch the heart and bow above the heart pocket. Embroider the bride's and groom's initials either side of the small heart.

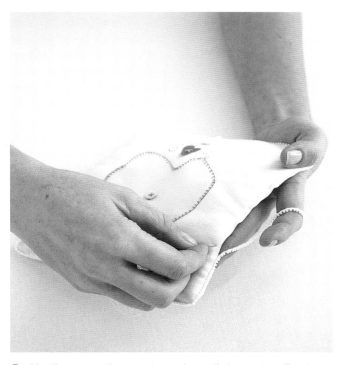

4 Fill the pillow with dried lavender. You may find it helps to roll a sheet of paper into a cone, then insert the tip through the gap in the side seam of the cushion and pour the lavender in through the top.

5 Neatly sew up the opening with small slipstitches. Finish by hand-sewing the decorative trimming around all four sides of the pillow, again using small slipstitches worked in a matching sewing thread.

Keepsakes

Months of planning, weeks of anticipation, hopes, fears, and endless listmaking will all culminate in a whirlwind of excitement when your wedding day finally arrives. Make sure that you, your family, and your friends remember every joyous moment of the celebrations by collecting together all the ephemera—snapshots, official pictures, menu cards, and messages—in specially made photograph albums and guest books, and sending out individual acknowledgments to each of your guests.

thank-you notes

It is a matter of politeness to send a card or letter to each of your guests on your return from honeymoon, or soon after the wedding, to thank them for attending the ceremony and to express your appreciation for any gifts they have given you. These notes should be handwritten, and taking the time to handmake the cards is further proof of your gratitude for their kindness and good wishes.

ABOVE LEFT Interesting leaves adorn handmade cards.

LEFT The edge of a doily makes a decorative mount for a white-bordered sepia photograph.

TOP RIGHT Print out small-scale versions of your favorite photo— a formal group or an off-guard moment caught by your best friend. Trim them down and fix to manilla card stock with photo corners.

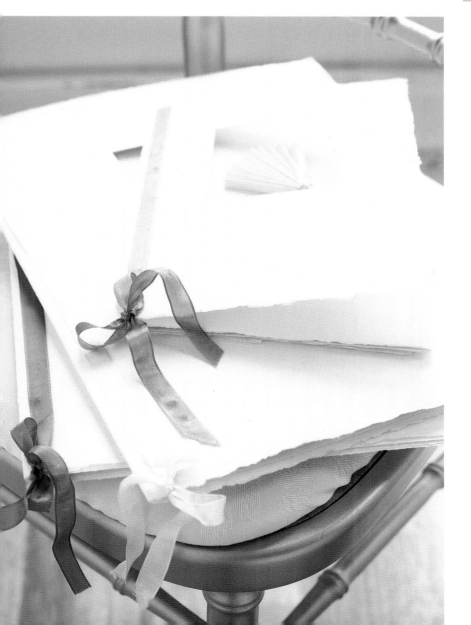

ABOVE LEFT If you have the time, you can make each card to its own individual design, rather than mass-producing them.

ABOVE CENTER A close-up photograph of your wedding bouquet is a wonderful image for a thank-you card. Black-and-white or sepia prints have a timeless air, and monochrome prints can always be made from colored images.

ABOVE RIGHT Write your letters on sheets of beautifully textured handmade rag paper, then roll them up and secure with a blob of colored sealing wax. Stamp the wax with your new initial for a traditional finishing touch.

LEFT To make these understatedly elegant cards, fold a rectangle of deckle-edged handmade paper in half and, using a scalpel, cut a square window in the center front. Tie a length of ribbon in a bow close to the crease and glue a small souvenir—a fan of paper, a dried flower, or a confetti petal—on the inside of the card, so it is clearly visible through the window.

PROJECT 11
guest book

Guest books provide a lasting memento of this very special occasion that will be treasured for years. They are also a wonderful way of giving friends and relations the opportunity to express their own thoughts and wishes for the bride and groom. Leave the book on a table in a quiet corner of the reception room or a side room, along with a pen, so that guests will have time to sit, reflect, and write a personal message. Either put up a small sign or ask one of your attendants to direct guests to the book table and ask everybody to make an entry.

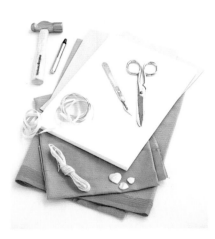

MATERIALS & EQUIPMENT
2 sheets of thick cardboard • Tape measure or yardstick
Pencil • Scissors • Fabric for cover
Contrasting fabric for lining
Embroidery needle • Stranded embroidery floss • Button
Double-sided Scotch tape • Self-adhesive dots
3 yards of narrow ribbon
¹/₂in stack of paper, the same size as the cardboard
Professional hole punch

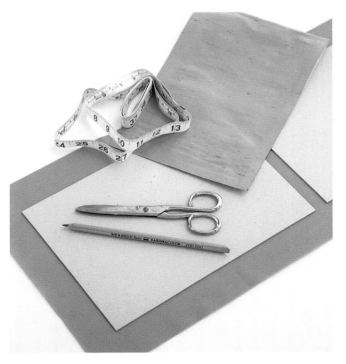

1   The fabric cover must be 3in deeper than the cardboard and twice its length plus 4in. The lining is ³/₄in less than the depth and twice the length, plus ³/₄in. For 8 x 10in paper you need 11 x 28in cover fabric and 7 x 24in of lining.

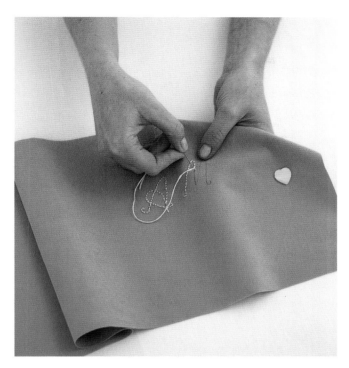

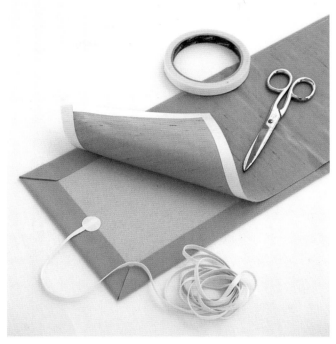

2 Mark the position for the initials on the front (leave 1½in for the hems at the top and right edges), then draw them in. Sew over the lines in running stitch using the embroidery floss. Sew the button 2in from the center-right edge.

3 Tape the cover fabric to the pieces of cardboard. Turn over 1½in at each edge and leave a ¾in gap between the boards for the spine. Miter the corners. Anchor 1 yard of ribbon to the front edge. Tape on the lining, leaving a ¾in margin.

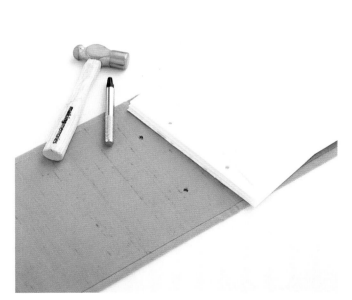

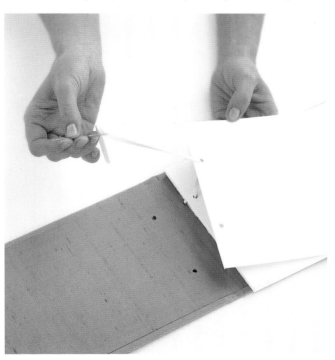

4 Punch two holes through the stack of paper, ½in from one edge. Make two holes in corresponding positions on the front and back covers. Use an office punch for the paper and an awl to pierce the cardboard.

5 Cut the remaining ribbon into two equal lengths. Thread them through the holes in the paper, then through the front and back covers. Tie loosely in position, so the book can open easily, then finish each ribbon with a bow.

ABOVE LEFT AND ABOVE A set of matching albums, like these beautiful handbound volumes, will hold honeymoon souvenirs, tickets, brochures, and other printed ephemera.

LEFT Label your storage boxes neatly for easy reference.

keepsakes

Those once vital checklists, guest lists, swatches, tear sheets, magazine articles, and other paraphernalia that you accumulated when planning your wedding will all acquire their own special meaning in time. Preserve your memories by sorting them into carefully labeled scrapbooks, boxes, and files, for even the tiniest scrap of wrapping paper or scrawled love note will one day be an irreplaceable and sentimental keepsake. You can also allocate separate storage boxes for your wedding cards, letters, and the photographs that didn't quite make it into the albums.

ABOVE A simple tie-up portfolio, either bought or made from a folded sheet of mounting board and trimmed with contrasting corners and spine, is the best way to store large presentation photographs, mood boards, or sketches for your wedding dress. Make a label bearing the date of your wedding or your monograms.

LEFT Turn your favorite bits and pieces into a nostalgic artwork. Glue rows of luggage labels to a plain stretched canvas (available from good art supply stores), then display photos, a sachet of rice, beads, buckles, dried flowers, and ribbon samples by tying them onto the strings.

PROJECT 12
scrapbook

After a wedding, there is always a huge stack of ephemera. In addition to all the cards and photographs, there are endless bits and pieces, all of which have their own particular significance—from receipts and brochures to pressed flowers, fabric swatches, and gift tags. Keep them all safe and sound in this pretty fabric-covered scrapbook, and group items together to make pages of particular memories. Label and caption everything so you can look back and remember all those significant details in years to come.

MATERIALS & EQUIPMENT
Spiral-bound scrapbook • Ruler or tape measure
Linen fabric for the cover • Fabric for the lining
Scissors • Double-sided Scotch tape
18in length of medium-width ribbon • Self-adhesive dots
Scraps of harmonizing cotton fabric and felt
Selection of buttons, sequins, and ribbon
Matching embroidery thread • Fabric glue
White fabric

1   For the cover you will need a rectangle of fabric 1½in deeper than your scrapbook and 1¾in wider than the open book. Apply a length of double-sided tape to the wrong side of each edge and fold over, short edges first.

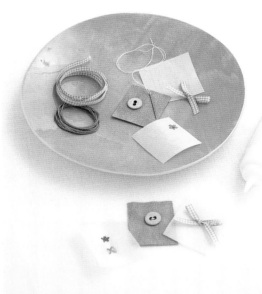

2 Cut the ribbon in two halves and trim the ends. Stick a piece to the center front and back using adhesive dots. Cut two rectangles of lining fabric $^3/_4$in shorter and $^1/_2$in wider than the inside cover and anchor them with double-sided tape.

3 Cut six patches from the scraps of fabric, in various sizes from 1 x 1$^1/_2$in rectangles to 1$^1/_2$in squares. Sew a button to one and flower sequins to another. Tie a length of narrow ribbon in a small bow and sew it to the third patch.

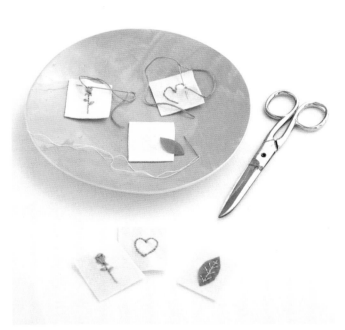

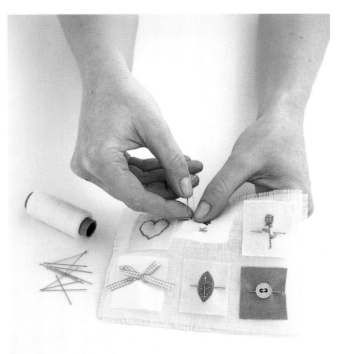

4 Cut a felt leaf and sew it on to the fourth patch with contrasting embroidery thread to form a pattern of veins. Stitch a small pink heart outline and a tiny rosebud with a green stem on the remaining patches.

5 Cut a rectangle of white fabric, approximately 5 x 10in. Fray the edges, then pin the patches in place. Stitch them down with matching sewing thread. Glue the panel to the front of the scrapbook with a thin layer of fabric glue.

sources

CAKES

CAKE DIVAS
By appointment only;
call 310-399-2499
www.cakedivas.com
Upscale custom cakes, from
classic elegance to over-the-
top whimsy.

CHERYL KLEINMAN
448 Atlantic Avenue
Brooklyn, NY 11217
By appointment only;
call 718-237-2271

CONFETTI CAKES
102 West 87th Street
New York, NY 10024
By appointment only;
call 212-877-9580.
www.confetticakes.com
Sculptural, still-life designs.

JAN KISH LA PETITE FLEUR
P.O. Box 872
Columbus, OH 43085
By appointment;
call 614-848-5855
www.jankishlapetitefleur.com
Cakes and sweet accessories.

MIKE'S AMAZING CAKES
14820 NE 31st Circle
Redmond, WA 98052
By appointment only;
call 425-869-2992
www.mikesamazingcakes.com
Off-beat, unconventional cakes.

RON BEN-ISRAEL
42 Greene Street
New York, NY 10013
By appointment only;
call 212-625-3369
www.weddingcakes.com
Unique wedding cakes.

SWEET LADY JANE
8360 Melrose Avenue
Los Angeles, CA 90069
323-653-3771
www.sweetladyjane.com
Fresh fruit cakes.

**SYLVIA WEINSTOCK
CAKES LTD.**
273 Church Street
New York, NY 10013
By appointment only;
call 212-925-6698
www.sylviaweinstock.com
Full-size and miniature cakes.

CONFETTI

BRIDALINK
www.bridalink.com
Confetti personalized with your
names or initials.

CONFOTI
www.confoti.com
Each piece of confetti displays
a photo.

JEAN M ESSENTIALS
Call 800-766-8595 or visit
www.jeanmessentials to
request a catalog.
Bubbles, rice, lavender, and
birdseed, as well as favors.

KEEPSAKE FAVORS
www.keepsakefavors.com
Real freeze-dried rose petals.
Also decorative place cards
and table cards.

ROMANTIC FLOWERS
www.romanticflowers.com
Silk rose petals, ribbons, and
paper for making cone-shaped
holders. Also candles and
favors.

TOPS MALIBU
www.topsmalibu.com
Butterfly-shaped paper
confetti, plus bottles of
bubbles, mini sparklers,
and pennants.

WEDDING FAVORS

BEAUCOUP
www.beau-coup.com
Wedding and bridal shower
favors, including candles,
sachets, soaps, silver
keepsakes, and custom-
designed cookies.

BELLATERRA
www.bellaterra.net
Exquisite packaging and
invitation design, as well as
well-priced flower seeds,
candy tins, matches, and
CD covers.

BEVERLY CLARK
Call 800-888-6866 or visit
www.beverlyclark.com for a
retailer near you.
Cake boxes and other
presentation ideas.

CRABTREE & EVELYN
Visit www.crabtree-evelyn.com
for a retailer near you.
Their miniature soaps, bath
gels, and other toiletries are
perfect for bridal showers.

CONFETTI
www.confetti-event.com
Gorgeous boxes and custom-
monogrammed tags, plus
hand-dipped pretzel sticks and
pink French meringues.

GODIVA
Visit www.godiva.com for a
retailer near you.
Two- or four-chocolate
assortments in gold ballotins
with pretty ribbons and
decorative treatments.

MY OWN LABELS
www.myownlabels.com
Personalized labels and hang-
tags, plus Chinese take-out
boxes, burlap bags, heart-
shaped tins, and more.

PEARL RIVER
www.pearlriver.com
Colorful, stylish, and affordable
Chinese imports, from paper
decorations and lacquered
chopsticks to quirky candies
and satin pincushions.

VOSGES HAUT-CHOCOLAT
520 North Michigan Avenue
Chicago, IL 60611
Call 888-301-9688 or visit
www.vosgeschocolate.com for
details of a retailer near you.
Chic chocolate treats, including
the 'Sophie' bars, which are
ideal for bridal showers.

WEDDING THINGS
www.weddingthings.com
Stylish keepsakes and
packaging, including affordable
monogrammed items.

INVITATIONS & STATIONERY

ARAK KANOFSKY STUDIOS
Call 610-599-1161 or visit
www.arakkanofskystudios.com
for a retailer near you.
Custom-designed invitations
featuring hand-painted details,
exquisite calligraphy, and luxe
ribbons and paper.

CARLSON CRAFT
Call 800-774-6848 or visit
www.carlsoncraft.com for a
retailer near you.
Well-priced designs offering
traditional styles as well as
more unconventional looks—
whimsical palettes, fonts,
and shapes.

CARROT & STICK PRESS
6020A Adeline Street, Suite C
Oakland, CA 94608
510-595-5353
www.carrrotandstickpress.com
Charming, letterpress-printed
place cards, stationery gifts,
and invitations.

CHELSEA PAPER
www.chelseapaper.com
Online paperie representing
wedding invitation companies.

CRANE'S
Visit www.crane.com for
a retailer near you.
Traditional, elegant invitations,
plus do-it-yourself wedding
stationery, providing everything
you need to computer print
your own invitations.

KATE'S PAPERIE
561 Broadway
New York, NY 10012
212-941-9816
www.katespaperie.com.
Representing distinguished
invitation lines, plus print-them-
yourself supplies.

PAPER GIRL
2158 Lawton Street
Fullerton, CA 92833
By appointment only;
714-446-9503
www.paper-girl.com
Exquisite, hip, handmade
invitations.

PULP INVITATIONS
Call 800-371-1796 or visit
www.pulpinvitations.com for
a retailer near you.
Stark, muted palette; smart
save-the-date styles.

SOOLIP PAPERIE & PRESS
8646 Melrose Avenue
West Hollywood, CA 90069
Call 310-360-0545 or visit
www.soolip.com for a retailer
near you.
Custom letterpress and a
wedding papers collection.

SNOW & GRAHAM
Call 773-665-9000 or visit
www.snowandgraham.com
for a retailer near you.
Stylish, modern, minimalist
designs. Excellent for bridal
shower or bachelorette party
invitations.

WILLIAM ARTHUR
Visit www.williamarthur.com
for a retailer near you.
Traditional, understated,
stationery with a contemporary
twist.

BRIDAL FABRICS, DECORATIVE ACCESSORIES AND SEWING NOTIONS

BLANKS FABRICS
6709 Whitestone Road
Baltimore, MD 21207
410-944-0040
www.blanksfab.com
Bridal and specialty fabrics.

THE CAROL HARRIS COMPANY
1265 South Main
Dyersburg, TN 38024
713-285-9419
www.carolharrisco.com
Swiss, French, and English
laces and trims, as well as a
limited selection of vintage
fabrics and lace, and a good
selection of mother-of-pearl
buttons.

CONSO PRODUCTS
www.conso.com
Decorative trims, upholstery
braid, and opulent tassels.

JO-ANN FABRIC
Visit www.joannfabric.com for
your nearest store.
Well-priced fabrics, sewing
supplies, and embellishments.

KATE'S PAPERIE
140 W 57th St
New York, NY
212-459-0700
www.katespaperie.com
Ribbons, paper
embellishments, boxes, and
little bags.

M&J TRIMMINGS
www.mjtrim.com
Rhinestones, sequined flowers,
ribbons, lace, rosettes, beaded
braid, and fur and feather trims,
all to buy online.

MICHAEL'S
Visit www.michaels.com for
your nearest store.
Craft supplies for favors, veils,
silk flowers, and beads.

MIDORI
Visit www.midoriribbon.com for
a retailer near you.
Luxe ribbons (velvet, taffeta,
dupioni silk, and dotted
organdy).

MOKUBA
55 West 39th Street
New York, NY 10018
212-869-8900
www.mokubany.com
43,000 ribbon styles and trims.

NICHOLAS KNIEL
290 Hilderbrand Avenue
Atlanta, GA 30328
404-252-8825
www.nicholaskniel.com
Exquisite mother-of-pearl, shell
inlay, and fabric-covered
buttons. Also fabric flowers,
ribbon roses, and vintage
ribbons.

REPRO DEPOT FABRICS
www.reprodepot.com
Ribbons and trims from all over
the world, including cute
vintage-style ribbons.

THE RIBBONERIE
191 Portrero Avenue
San Francisco, CA 94103
415-626-6184
www.theribbonerie.com
Ribbons of all descriptions—
wire-edged, jacquard, velvet,
grosgrain, metallic, and even
glorious vintage examples

TINSEL TRADING CO.
47 West 38th Street
New York, NY 10018
212-730-1030
www.tinseltrading.com
Vintage buttons and beads, as
well as gorgeous silk and
velvet flowers, sequins, metallic
tassels, and exquisite ribbons.

ART AND CRAFT SUPPLIES

B. B. CRAFTS
www.bbcrafts.com
Spools of organza ribbon,
organza drawstring bags in
a rainbow of colours, and tulle
by the roll.

THE CRAFT PLACE
www.thecraftplace.com
Craft basics, such as glitter,
glue, and floral tape.

SAVE ON CRAFTS
www.save-on-crafts.com
Wedding supplies, including
silk flowers, silk rose petals,
Jordan almonds, dried
rosebuds and petals, dried
lavender, favor boxes, and
ribbons.

YOUNGER AND SON
595 Maple Avenue
Lansdale, PA 19446
215-362-2828
www.youngerson.com
Floral foam in a huge variety of
different forms. Also floating
candles, Cellophane, ribbons,
and packaging for favors.

FLORAL AND EVENT DESIGN

ARTFOOL
161 Allen Street
New York, NY 10002
212-253-2737
www.artfool.com
Creative, sophisticated, and
unique event planning and
floral design.

AVI ADLER
87 Luquer Street
Brooklyn, NY 11231
718-243-0804
www.aviadler.com
Whimsical, inventive, anything-
but-typical event planning and
wedding flowers.

BELLE FLEUR
134 Fifth Avenue
New York, NY 10011
212-254-8703
www.bellefleurny.com
Elegant, modern, wedding
flowers.

GORDON MORRIS EVENT
PLANNING & FLORAL
DESIGN
7801 Melrose Avenue, #5
Los Angeles, CA 90046
323-653-0065
Unique, cutting-edge flower
arrangements.

LOVE, LUCK & ANGELS
213-842-9952
www.loveluckandangels.com
Handles celebrity clients as
well as budget-minded
couples.

MARK'S GARDEN
13838 Ventura Boulevard
Sherman Oaks, CA 91423
818-906-1718
Specializing in lavish and
exuberant "L.A.-fabulous"
designs.

MUDD FLEURS
66 E Walton 1st Floor
Chicago, IL 60611
312-337-6883
Exquisite and unusual flowers
for sophisticated, upscale
weddings.

THE PERFECT PETAL
3615 W 32nd Ave
Denver, CO 80211
800-241-3418
www.theperfectpetal.com
Dramatic imported flowers and
innovative arrangements with a
modern approach.

TAKASHIMAYA
693 5th Avenue
New York, NY 10022
212-350-0111
Upscale Japanese department
store with an Eastern-
influenced aesthetic. The
ground-floor floral boutique
offers glorious flowers,
including large salmon-pink
peonies (in season).

LINENS AND OTHER RENTALS

DURKIN AWNING
CORPORATION
90 Beaver Brook Road
Danbury, CT 06810
800-498-3028
Striped awnings and fancy
white tents.

ROBERTA KARSCH-
RESOURCE ONE
818-343-3451
www.resourceone.info
Fine table linen, chair
treatments, and table
accessories; ships nationwide.

RUTH FISCHL
141 West 28th Street
New York, New York 10001
212-273-9710
www.ruthfischl.com
Fine linens, canopies, arches,
and vases.

SNYDER
843-766-3366
www.snydereventrentals.com
Ballroom chairs, shepherd
hooks, tiki torches, and even
dance floors.

TAYLOR RENTAL
www.taylorrental.com
Everything for a wedding party,
from candelabras to cotton
candy machines.

templates

To make a template, either use a photocopier to copy the desired template onto heavy paper, or trace the pattern and transfer it to heavy paper or card stock. Cut out the template, pin it to the wrong side of your fabric, then cut out. You can trace round the template in faint pencil if preferred.

picture credits

Key: ph= photographer, a=above, b=below, r=right, l=left, c=center

All projects photographed by Carolyn Barber. All other photographs by Polly Wreford unless otherwise stated.

Page 1 etched crystal goblets from Evertrading, spiral plates from Designers Guild, damask tablecloth from Antique Linen Company, pink and blue damask napkins from Thomas Goode; 2 condiments, flatware, and place-card holders from Thomas Goode, Stuart Crystal wineglasses from Waterford Crystal, china from Richard Ginori; 3 & 4 ph Carolyn Barber; 5 rustic wire basket from Fenwick, handmade paper from Paperchase, white fabric petals from Confetti, wire-edge ribbon from VV Rouleaux; 6 cake box from Bomboniere, fabric flower from VV Rouleaux; 8 three-tiered cake decorated with icing pearls designed by Eric at Savoir Design, pink satin ribbon from VV Rouleaux; 10 all & 11bl ph Craig Fordham; 11ar 28 Portland Place, London; 12al 28 Portland Place, London; 12br braided fabric and pearl-headed dressmaker's pins from John Lewis; 12–13a, 13ar, 13br, 14, 15 all ph Craig Fordham; 18–19 all ph Craig Fordham except 18ac; 20ac, 20–21a, 20–21b, 21ac & 21ar all ph Craig Fordham; 24al 28 Portland Place, London, flatware and pot from Christofle UK Ltd, crystal wineglass from Evertrading; 24–25 etched goblets from Oka, flatware from IKEA; 26l Skywood House, Middlesex, designed by architect Graham Phillips, cups and saucers from Wedgwood, similar cylindrical glass flower vase available from IKEA or Habitat, blue-rimmed china from Royal Worcester, four-tiered cake from Savoir Design; 26ar shot glasses from Habitat; 28al crystal wineglass from Evertrading; 28ar etched crystal goblets from Evertrading, spiral plates from Designers Guild, damask tablecloth from Antique Linen Company, pink and blue damask napkins from Thomas Goode; 29 floral china table setting from Richard Ginori, engraved goblet set from Evertrading, shallow silver vase from Kenneth Turner, chairs from Nordic Style; 30br chairs and cushions from Nordic Style; 31br 28 Portland Place, London; 34 cake from Savoir Design, pearl-beaded braid from VV Rouleaux; 36l cakes from Savoir Design; 36r cake from Savoir Design, pearl-beaded braid and organza chiffon flower from VV Rouleaux, crystal champagne flutes from William Yeoward Crystal, china from Royal Worcester; 37 Skywood House, Middlesex designed by architect Graham Phillips/four-tiered cake decorated with icing pearls designed by Eric at Savoir Design; 39l cake from Savoir Design; 39r cake designed by Makiko Sakita at Confetti; 40a cake from Savoir Design, paper butterflies from C. Best at Nine Elms Market, Vauxhall, gold-striped ribbon and sequined butterflies from VV Rouleaux, gold-rimmed glassware from Thomas Goode; 40b embroidered linen coasters from the Irish Linen Company; 41 cakes from Savoir Design; 43 cakes from Waitrose, pie fork from Antique Designs Ltd; 44 napkin holder decoration from VV Rouleaux; 45a napkins and gilt hoop napkin rings from Thomas Goode; 45bc silver fretwork napkin rings from Grange, pewter bowl from Kenneth Turner; 45br silver-rimmed china from Royal Worcester; 46a embroidered napkins from Antique Designs Ltd; 46b white porcelain rose napkin ring from Thomas Goode; 47al damask napkin and beaded tassel napkin holder from Thomas Goode, patterned plates from Christofle; 47ar silk tassels with mink pompoms (made to hold keys) used as napkin holders from Robbie Spina; 47c scalloped plates from Designers Guild, flower braid napkin holder from Jane Churchill; 48, 49a, 49bl & 49bc all ph David Loftus; 49br patterned china from Richard Ginori, blue etched glass plate from IKEA; 52al champagne flutes from Evertrading; 52ar handmade paper from Paperchase; 52b spotty cups and saucers from Richard Ginori; 54ar porcelain bunny place-card holder from Herend Porcelain; 58b crystal cakestand from Baccarat, green glass balls from Paperchase; 59br patterned china and silver coffeepot from Christofle; 62 flower and beaded garland candleholder from VV Rouleaux; 63 cream-painted wire baskets from Fenwick; 67ar glass tealight holders from Habitat, mirror from C. Best at Nine Elms Market, Vauxhall; 67br tray edged with glass beads and frosted glass votive holders from Fenwick; 68ar glass lanterns from R.K. Alliston; 69al fretwork lantern from Fenwick; 69ac white wire lantern from Fenwick; 69ar glass candleholders from Menu A/S; 69b Chinese lanterns from IKEA; 72 similar favor boxes available from Confetti and Bomboniere, plate from Habitat; 74ar & br truffles and gold-wrapped chocolate hearts all from Rococo chocolates; 75 handmade cookies from Savoir Designs; 78a similar favor boxes from Confetti and Bomboniere; 79al corrugated favor boxes from Bomboniere, ribbons from VV Rouleaux; 80al candy-pink favor box from Paperchase, ribbon from VV Rouleaux, floral gold-rimmed plates from Royal Worcester; 80ac colored etched wineglass from William Yeoward Crystal, ribbon from VV Rouleaux; 80cr wire garland of tiny glass hearts from VV Rouleaux; 80b all plates and translucent onyx bowl from Thomas Goode; 80–81a white bone china from Royal Copenhagen, embroidered handkerchief from the Irish Linen Company; 81ac Sandringham plate from Royal Worcester, floral handkerchief from the Irish Linen Company; 81ar galvanized metal plant pot from the Netherlands Flower Bulb Information Center; 81b ribbon and silk flower from VV Rouleaux, gold box from Paperchase, gold-rimmed china from Royal Worcester; 84 rustic wire basket from Fenwick, handmade paper from Paperchase, white fabric petals from Confetti, wire-edge ribbon from VV Rouleaux; 86ac flower-petal confetti from Confetti; 86-87a flower-petal confetti from Confetti, white-painted wire basket from Fenwick; 88b embroidered linen sachets and embroidered table linen from the Irish Linen Company; 90al embroidered silk bags from Grange.